LIGHT SWITCH

Dave Osmundsen

BROADWAY PLAY PUBLISHING INC
New York
www.broadwayplaypub.com
info@broadwayplaypub.com

LIGHT SWITCH
© Copyright 2022 Dave Osmundsen

Cover art by Bay McCulloch

First edition: May 2022
I S B N: 978-0-88145-933-3

Book design: Marie Donovan
Page make-up: Adobe InDesign
Typeface: Palatino

LIGHT SWITCH received its world premiere
with Spectrum Theatre Ensemble (Clay Martin,
Artistic Director) on 22 April 2022 as a part of the
Neurodiversity Everywhere Tour (Will Stanley, Tour
Manager). The cast and creative contributors were:

HENRY ....Daniel Perkins
ROGGIE .... Teddy Lytle
JOSEPH .... Brian Harrison
MARIAN.. Karin Trachtenberg
AARON/KEN/ANOTHER GUY........................ Adam Bram

Director.. Allen MacLeod
Stage management............... Bay McCulloch & Jay Walker
Intimacy/fight choreography............................. Teddy Lytle
Costume design.. Kat Fortner
Set design............................Max Ponticelli & Will Stanley
Lighting design ....Sam Mosher
Technical direction.. Dan Kurtz

CHARACTERS

HENRY, *gay and autistic, 8-28, male*
ROGGIE, *his roommate, gay. Pronounced like "Roger", but*
with an "ee". 21-28, male
JOSEPH, *gay, 29, male*
MARIAN, HENRY's *mother, 33-54, female*
AARON, *a boy* HENRY *used to play with, 11, male*
KEN, *a student, 20, male*
ANOTHER GUY, *gay, 23, male*

Casting Note: AARON, KEN, *and* ANOTHER GUY *are played*
by the same actor. I affectionally call this the "Other Guy
Track." :-)

STAGING NOTE

The play jumps back and forth through time and space over the span of 20 years. The actor playing HENRY will have to make the most changes. I encourage directors to come up with their own creative transitions from one scene into the next in terms of costume/hair changes for HENRY.

ACT ONE

Scene One

(A playground at an elementary school. April 2001. HENRY, *age 11, runs around the playground.)*

HENRY: Heathcliff! Heathcliff! Where are you, Heathcliff!? You are my love! My life!
Be with me always—take any form—drive me mad! Only do not leave me in this abyss, where I cannot find you! Oh, God! It is unutterable! I can not live without my life! I can not live without my soul!
Heathcliff! HEATHCLIFF!!!

*(*AARON, *age 11, enters, playing "Heathcliff". He is not very enthusiastic.)*

AARON: Catherine, Catherine.
You teach me now how cruel you've been—cruel and false. Why did you despise me? Why did you betray your own heart, Cathy? I have not one word of comfort. You deserve this. You have killed yourself.

HENRY: Oh Heathcliff, Linton couldn't love me as much as you can.
My love for Linton is like the foliage in the woods: time will change it, I'm well aware, as winter changes the trees. My love for you resembles the eternal rocks beneath: a source of little visible delight, but necessary.
Kiss me, Heathcliff!

AARON: Can we play something else?

HENRY: No.
Kiss me, Heathcliff!

AARON: I don't want to.

HENRY: I don't care. Kiss me, Heathcliff!

(HENRY *tries to kiss* AARON. AARON *rather violently pushes* HENRY *off of him.*)

HENRY: Owww!

AARON: I told you I didn't want to.

HENRY: You didn't have to push me like that.

AARON: You also don't *kiss people* when they *don't want to be kissed.*

HENRY: I wasn't *really* going to kiss you. I was going to *pretend* to kiss you.

AARON: Don't you wanna play kickball instead?

HENRY: No. I'd rather play "Wuthering Heights."
If you'd like, I can play Heathcliff and you can play Cathy. She has all the better lines anyway.

AARON: I don't want to play Cathy.

HENRY: Okay, then what do you want to play? We can play "Jane Eyre." Or "Pride and Prejudice." Or "Tess of the d'Urbervilles." Or what about "Oliver Twist"? That doesn't involve kissing.

AARON: I said I wanted to play kickball.

HENRY: No you didn't.

AARON: Yes I did!

HENRY: You asked if I wanted to play kickball, I said no. You did not indicate in that sentence that you actually wanted to play kickball.

AARON: Well I do.

HENRY: And I don't. Kickball is boring. And I always kick the ball too hard and someone always catches it and I always get out.

AARON: I told you. You gotta kick it softly. Then they have to actually run and get the ball and by the time they reach it, you're already at first base.

HENRY: That's when I get a foul ball.

AARON: That's because you kick it too far to the side. Come on, I can teach you—

HENRY: No! I wanna play "Wuthering Heights"!

AARON: We're not going to play "Wuthering Heights" today! We're going to play kickball!

HENRY: Says who!?

AARON: Says I. I don't want to play games about books I haven't even read before.

HENRY: You've seen the movies though.

AARON: Yes. That's *all we watch* whenever I come over.

HENRY: I thought you liked them.

AARON: I do…

HENRY: So why don't we continue playing—

AARON: Because everyone else laughs at us. You know that, right?

HENRY: I do know. And I don't care. They're all imbecilic, anyway.

AARON: They think we're…*boyfriends*!!!

HENRY: But you have a crush on Katherine Steinhardt.

AARON: Well she, and others, think we're like, *going out*. Like on *dates*.

HENRY: I don't understand how anyone can think that.

AARON: …Really?

HENRY: Yes.

AARON: ...Do I *really* have to explain this to you?

HENRY: Yes.

AARON: Catherine and Heathcliff are going out, right?

HENRY: Not exactly.

AARON: Well...Elizabeth and Mr Darcy are going out... right?

HENRY: Again, not exactly.

AARON: Tess and Angel ! They're going out...right?

HENRY: They get married and he leaves her, so no, not exactly.

AARON: But they all...*love*...each other, right?

HENRY: Catherine and Heathcliff do. Elizabeth and Darcy hate each other at first, then they do after she sees how big and fancy his house is. Tess and Angel do, but he doesn't like that she's *done it* with other men before, even though she *did it* with Alec *against her will.*

AARON: Okay, but you get my point, right?

HENRY: No. None of those characters are going out.

AARON: We play games where people *love* each other, so other people think that *we* love each other. *You* and *I.*

HENRY: But I do love you, Aaron. You're my best friend.

AARON: I mean the *other* kind of love.

HENRY: Like the one my parents had before my dad left?

AARON: ...*Yeah.*

HENRY: I love you that way too, Aaron.

AARON: What?

HENRY: I dared not tell you, because I feared how it would impact our friendship. And because you had a crush on Katherine Steinhardt. But I do love you, Aaron. Most ardently.

(Pause. REALLY awkward pause.)

AARON: So you want to…*actually* kiss me?

HENRY: I've thought about it! But I dared not!
I was, however, going to give you a gift.
(He pulls out a small paperback copy of Wuthering Heights. *He holds it out to* AARON.*)*
Your very own copy of *Wuthering*—

*(*AARON *slams the book to the ground.)*

AARON: You know the only reason we were friends was because my *mom made me*!? I never wanted to be friends with you.
All these games we played were *stupid*! And *you're* stupid! Don't talk to me again, you retarded faggot.

*(*AARON *runs off to play kickball.* HENRY *is alone for a few moments. He may or may not be about to cry.)*

(Before he can let the tears fall, he picks up and opens the copy of Wuthering Heights. *He sits on the ground and starts reading it.)*

Scene Two

(A private library in a very nice summer home in Upstate New York. August 2017)

(We see HENRY, *age 27, in the library. He is dressed in a buttoned down shirt tucked into his khaki pants. Perhaps he's a bit too dressed up for the occasion. He's reading an old, tattered copy of Thackeray's* Vanity Fair *that he picked up from the bookshelf.)*

(After a few moments of this, the door opens and JOSEPH *enters.* HENRY *keeps his eyes to his book. His concentration is outstanding.)*

JOSEPH: Oh sorry. Didn't realize anyone was in here.

*(*HENRY *keeps reading.* JOSEPH *looks at him.)*

JOSEPH: Enjoying the book?

*(*HENRY *keeps reading. Awkward silence. A few moments later,* HENRY *closes the book.)*

HENRY: I apologize. I was waiting to reach the end of the chapter. I don't like stopping books in the middle of chapters because I don't like the feeling of something being incomplete.
Hello.
I'm reading *Vanity Fair* by William Makepeace Thackeray.

JOSEPH: Hi there.
Wasn't that a movie with, what's her face…

HENRY: Reese Witherspoon.

JOSEPH: Yeah. I saw that a while ago. Kinda boring, I thought.

HENRY: Yes. That version is terrible. There are a lot of other miniseries adaptations of it that are much better. I also saw a stage adaptation of it earlier this year.

JOSEPH: Cool.

HENRY: The book was released in 1848 in a 19-part serialized version with the subtitle *Pen and Pencil Sketches of English Society* and then it was published in one volume. It had the subtitle of *A Novel Without A Hero.*

JOSEPH: You…know a lot about it.

HENRY: Yes. The Victorian era is my favorite literary era. I'm actually getting my Ph.D in 19th Century British Literature from Columbia University.

JOSEPH: Fancy. I barely got my Bachelor's Degree.

HENRY: You mean you *got* your Bachelor's Degree. You either did or you didn't.

JOSEPH: I mean I *did*, but not like, with any of those Latin things...

HENRY: I got *summa cum laude* for my Bachelor's Degree in English. I went to Montclair State University in New Jersey. Then I got my Master's in English at Columbia, which, as I said, is where I am getting my PhD in 19th Century British Literature.

JOSEPH: Nice.
So you're into like, Jane Austen, or...?

HENRY: Jane Austen was actually Regency era. King George III was supposed to rule, but no one wanted him to, so his son ruled as regent, which is when someone rules in the stead of whomever is *technically* ruling.
That was from 1811 to 1820, then Queen Victoria took over. Jane Austen published *Emma* in 1815, a book with a main character whom she said no one but her would much like, and the Prince Regent decided to give her "the honor" of dedicating it to him, but she didn't like him because he was a pompous idiot. So her dedication read, "To His Royal Highness the Prince Regent, this work is, by His Royal Highness's permission, most respectfully dedicated by His Royal Highness's dutiful and obedient humble servant, the author." Which everyone thought was a huge insult to the Prince Regent.
But yes. I'm into Jane Austen.

JOSEPH: Okay.

HENRY: I'm actually writing my dissertation about her. Well, about her writing. It's called "The Spectrum of Austen: Portrayals and Presence of Autistic Characters in the novels of Jane Austen."

JOSEPH: Nice.

HENRY: You know whenever I go to one of these parties, I feel like I'm at a Jane Austen-esque ball. Except there are more people having sex.

JOSEPH: Oh?

HENRY: You have your "belles of the ball," the people all the men want to dance with. In this particular context, the strapping man every guy wants to have intercourse with. You have your wallflowers who are socially awkward and always wait to get asked to dance. In this context, wallflowers are the ones waiting for someone to ask them to sleep with them.
And then you have the ones who hate balls and would rather have stayed home but couldn't because their parents dragged them out hoping to find a potential suitor. That's me, which is why I am here in this library.

JOSEPH: Wait. Your *parents* brought you here?

HENRY: Oh no. My roommate Roggie did. He's off with a young man whose blue hair-dye is thinning out. I've only had sex once. He was inside me, which I didn't like. It didn't provide much comfort for me. I think I'd rather be inside someone. But I haven't tried it yet.

JOSEPH: Right…

Well. I'll let you get back to your reading.

HENRY: No. Please stay. I'll enjoy the company while Roggie is finishing up with that young man with the blue hair.

Besides, I've read this book twelve times.

(JOSEPH *laughs*.)

HENRY: That wasn't meant to be a joke. I really have read it twelve times.

JOSEPH: I know, just… You say it so matter of fact-ly, um… Sorry, what's your name?

(HENRY *holds out his hand*.)

HENRY: My name is Henry. Henry Sullivan.

JOSEPH: Joseph.

(JOSEPH *gives a little wave*. HENRY *still holds his hand out*.)

HENRY: Will you not shake my hand?

(JOSEPH *laughs, and shakes* HENRY's *hand*.)

HENRY: I must ask. Are you sure you would rather not be upstairs with another young man?

JOSEPH: I've had my fair share of that. I came down for a break, actually.

HENRY: This is where you come to take your breaks?

JOSEPH: Yep. Unspoken rule of this house is that this room is off limits to *any* sex-related act.

HENRY: How do you know that?

JOSEPH: Because this is *my* house.

HENRY: Wait a moment.

JOSEPH: Yep. This is my summer home, basically.

HENRY: So I've been reading in *your* library?

JOSEPH: Technically my uncle's. This is actually *his* summer house, but he's spending the summer in the Hamptons this year, so I'm using it.

HENRY: Does he know there are men having sex with each other?

JOSEPH: Nothing *he* hasn't done back in his heyday…

HENRY: That was meant to be a joke.

JOSEPH: Oh...

Sorry. Must've went, whoosh, right over my head.

HENRY: That happens a lot. My mother says I have a very esoteric sense of humor.

JOSEPH: Eccentric, definitely.

HENRY: No, eccentric means slightly strange. Esoteric means specific to a certain country or region. Or in this case, a certain people.

JOSEPH: You know your vocabulary.

HENRY: I know. I like to use it when I meet people for the first time. It helps me determine if they're imbeciles or not imbeciles.

JOSEPH: Which category do I fall into?

HENRY: Not an imbecile so far.

JOSEPH: Good...

(JOSEPH *begins to step towards* HENRY. HENRY *indicates the bookshelf.*)

HENRY: Have you read any of these books? Which one is your favorite?

JOSEPH: None of them.

HENRY: ...None? But...there are so many!

JOSEPH: I know. I like looking at them. Just...never had an interest in reading them.

HENRY: You should. There are some marvelous titles on these shelves.

JOSEPH: I'm sure. But my interest usually lies... elsewhere.

HENRY: By elsewhere, do you mean "sex"?

JOSEPH: Maybe...

(JOSEPH *steps towards* HENRY. HENRY *doesn't move. They lock eyes.* JOSEPH *looks at* HENRY. JOSEPH *then takes the book out of* HENRY's *hands.* HENRY *lets him. A moment of tension between them.*)

HENRY: You're very handsome, Joseph.

JOSEPH: Thanks.
May I touch you?

HENRY: Where?

JOSEPH: Just...in general.

HENRY: Are you going to put yourself inside of me?

JOSEPH: Only if you want me to.

HENRY: I don't.

JOSEPH: Then I won't.
But can I touch you?

HENRY: I'd like to know where.

JOSEPH: Your shoulder.

HENRY: Okay.

(JOSEPH *touches* HENRY's *shoulder.* HENRY *winces a little, but settles into it.*)

JOSEPH: Your neck.

HENRY: Okay.

(JOSEPH *touches* HENRY's *neck.* HENRY *winces a little, but settles into it.*)

JOSEPH: Your chest.

HENRY: Okay.

(JOSEPH *touches* HENRY's *chest, rubs his hand over it.* HENRY *winces a little, but settles into it.*)

JOSEPH: Your waist.

HENRY: No.

JOSEPH: Okay. Your face.

HENRY: Okay.

(JOSEPH *touches* HENRY's *face.* HENRY *doesn't wince at all. He and* JOSEPH *look each other in the eyes. A long, long, sustained moment between them. Perhaps they begin getting closer and closer to one another.*)

HENRY: I haven't...

JOSEPH: Haven't what?

HENRY: I haven't even gone out on a date with you.

JOSEPH: Does that mean we can't kiss?

HENRY: It means I...

(HENRY *falls into silence. He and* JOSEPH *look at each other again. Then:*)

HENRY: I wouldn't mind going on a date with you.

(*Long pause. Then, the door bursts open and* ROGGIE *enters, breaking the moment.*)

ROGGIE: Sorry.

HENRY: Roggie! I thought you were still with that gentleman with the blue hair.

ROGGIE: No, we finished like an hour ago. I was hooking up with someone else. You two busy, or...?

JOSEPH: Actually, I was about to check on upstairs, so... Having fun, Roggie?

ROGGIE: Yeah.

(JOSEPH *quickly goes to exit.*)

HENRY: It was nice to meet you, Joseph!

(JOSEPH *exits. A moment.* ROGGIE *looks after him and smiles at* HENRY.)

ROGGIE: Gee, Henry! You go to the *library* and the men are flocking to you! Hope I didn't ruin any sexual tension.

HENRY: You did.

ROGGIE: Sorry. I was gonna suggest we leave, but if you wanna stay, I totally get it.

HENRY: Do you think I should?

ROGGIE: Up to you. But I'm pretty sure you'll see Joseph around at another party this weekend.

HENRY: But I know not whether he'll *actually* show up to one.

ROGGIE: Then you can stay and wait for him.

HENRY: But I don't want to have to go back to the cabin by myself. Not at this time of night!

ROGGIE: Then come back to the cabin with me.

HENRY: But what if he comes back here?

ROGGIE: *Henry.* Do you wanna stay, or go?

(A moment)

HENRY: I'll go, for I am growing rather weary.But I do hope that Joseph and I shall meet again. I told him I wouldn't mind going out on a date with him. He didn't respond, but perhaps the next time I see him he'll agree to one.

(ROGGIE *is silent. Eerily so)*

HENRY: What is it, Roggie? Why are you silent?

ROGGIE: Nothing.

HENRY: Is it Joseph? Does he have a scandalous secret, like an insane lover hidden in the attic?

(ROGGIE *chuckles.)*

ROGGIE: No, nothing like that. I think.

HENRY: Then what is it?

ROGGIE: Joseph is…
Not really the kind who *dates*. You know what I mean?
He's a bit of a…

HENRY: Rapscallion?

ROGGIE: I wouldn't call him *that*. More like… Um…

HENRY: More like…? Please finish your sentence.

ROGGIE: Like…he likes to play the field.
A lot.
You know?

HENRY: I see.

ROGGIE: Yeah. I'm sorry, Henry. I don't mean to be a
downer. I just don't want you to get your hopes up for
something that probably won't happen.

(HENRY *is silent, clearly dejected.* ROGGIE *opens his arms.*
HENRY *nods.* ROGGIE *embraces him. A moment.*)

ROGGIE: Let's go back to the cabin. Okay?

(HENRY *nods.* ROGGIE *exits.* HENRY *places the copy of*
Vanity Fair *back on the bookshelf, and follows* ROGGIE *out
the door.*)

Scene Three

(*1998.* MARIAN, HENRY's *mother, and* HENRY, *age 8.*
They are watching the Gwyneth Paltrow version of Emma.
Silence as they watch)

(MARIAN *holds up a V H S of* Toy Story.)

MARIAN: You sure you don't wanna watch *Toy Story*?

HENRY: Yes I am sure.

(*Pause*)

MARIAN: How can an eight-year-old be interested in this? Can you even understand what they're saying?

HENRY: They're speaking English. Why wouldn't I understand them?

MARIAN: Are you even following this story?

(HENRY *pauses the movie.*)

HENRY: Yes. The blonde girl is named Emma. She was able to get her nanny married, so she thinks she can get other people married. So she tries to get her friend Harriet married to the pastor, but the pastor really wants Emma. And Mr Knightley doesn't like how Emma is forcing other people to get married, because she's playing with fate. But Emma keeps trying anyway, so she—

MARIAN: You can follow all that? That is remarkable.

HENRY: Not really. I just pay attention to the movie.

(*Pause.* HENRY *resumes the movie.*)

MARIAN: You know there's a book version of this, right?

HENRY: I know. I've read it.

MARIAN: Really?

HENRY: Yes. I checked it out of the library. You were with me. Remember?

MARIAN: You check out so many books I never know what you're reading.

HENRY: Oh yes. I've checked *Emma* out three times. I'll probably check it out a fourth time when we go to the library tomorrow.

MARIAN: It must be your favorite book, then.

HENRY: No. That's *The Woman in White.*

MARIAN: Oh yes. I remember you reading that.

HENRY: It's a mystery set in Victorian England about a man who meets a woman dressed in white whom he thinks is a ghost but—

MARIAN: Sssshhh. Let's keep watching the movie.

HENRY: You aren't even enjoying it.

MARIAN: Well you did such a good job summarizing the plot—

HENRY: I'm almost at where we are in the movie! So after Emma keeps trying to get Harriet with—

MARIAN: I'll catch up with it. Thank you.

HENRY: I wasn't finished. So anyway—

MARIAN: Listen to my tone, Henry. Do I sound like I want to hear you talk, or watch the movie?

HENRY: Watch the movie…

MARIAN: And we're *quiet* during movies, right?

HENRY: You weren't being quiet. You imbecilically asked me if I wanted to watch *Toy Story* a minute ago.

MARIAN: *(Getting up)* That's it. I'm turning this off.

(HENRY grabs the video case for Emma, *and clings on to it.)*

HENRY: No! Please don't, mommy! I didn't mean it! Honest!
Please, mommy. Don't turn off *Emma.*

(A moment. MARIAN looks at HENRY with the V H S box. She takes a few breaths.)

MARIAN: Okay. You're right. I should be quiet during movies, too.
But you can't call people imbeciles, Henry. I've told you, that's not nice.

HENRY: I'm sorry, mommy.

MARIAN: I forgive you, Henry.

Now do you *promise* me you'll be quiet the rest of the
movie?

HENRY: Can I say one more thing?

MARIAN: What, Henry?

HENRY: The main character in *The Woman in White* is
named Marian. That's your name, too.

(MARIAN *smiles.* HENRY *and* MARIAN *continue watching
the movie.*)

Scene Four

(*A cabin in Upstate New York. The evening after Scene
Two.* HENRY *is in his own bed reading* Great Expectations.
ROGGIE *is sitting in his bed in his underwear. He faces a
laptop. He is wrapping up a vlog post.*)

ROGGIE: So! In conclusion:
If someone is pressuring you into bareback, or
anything else you're uncomfortable with, it's okay to
say no. You will *not* be offending the other guy if you
do. And if he *is* offended, then he's not worth it to
begin with.
Remember: One night of *awesome* sex is not worth
waking up with something you'll have to live with for
the rest of your life.
Thanks for watching this episode of "Out and Around:
Sex and Dating Tips for Gay Men." I'm Roggie, and
if you want more sex and dating tips, click any of
the videos above, and be sure to *smash* that subscribe
button and click the bell for *all* the notifications!
Until next time, be sexy.
But most important, *be safe.* Byeee!
(*He closes his laptop. He stands up. Stretches. Then
examines his body.*)
You think this—

HENRY: I'm almost done with this chapter.
(A few moments. He reads, then closes the book.)
You may speak now.

ROGGIE: Does this underwear look good on me?

HENRY: It accentuates your covered and uncovered parts tremendously.

ROGGIE: *(Playful)* You could've said yes. Didn't have to be so ostentatious!

HENRY: An exemplary use of your vocabulary.

(ROGGIE starts putting on a T-shirt and shorts.)

ROGGIE: Why thank you! Did I tell you it got me laid last night? I told this guy with blue hair that his hair looked very "ebullient", he was flattered because he recognized me from my YouTube channel, then he—

HENRY: Proceeded to give you a most pleasurable blow job. Yes Roggie. You've already regaled me with this story.

ROGGIE: Maybe if I find one of those B D S M people, I can use the word "bellicose" on them!

HENRY: I would like to simultaneously watch and not watch the result of that exchange.

ROGGIE: You should start getting ready, too.

HENRY: Do you think Joseph will be there tonight? I haven't perished the thought of us possibly meeting again all day.

ROGGIE: You know there *are* gonna be other guys there who will *more than likely* want to hook up with you.

HENRY: I don't want a hook up. I want to continue my conversation with Joseph.

ROGGIE: No offense, but why are you still hung up on him?

HENRY: I still take offense to you asking that question.
That was meant to be a joke.
But if you must know, it's because he *talked* to me,
Roggie. Something that most men fail to even attempt.

ROGGIE: Remember Ken? He talked to you.

HENRY: And he turned out to be an imbecile. Joseph
might not be an imbecile.
In any case, I shall not be going out with you tonight if
you cannot guarantee Joseph's presence.

ROGGIE: You know I can't, Henry.

HENRY: Then I shan't come out with you. I'm going to
stay in and catch up on my summer reading.

ROGGIE: Henry. I brought you upstate to get *laid*. By a
human. Not by books.

HENRY: I much prefer books to humans. I find them
more engaging and trustworthy company.

(HENRY *opens his book and starts reading.* ROGGIE *takes the
book from* HENRY *and closes it shut.)*

ROGGIE: Well then, I hope you remember your place!

HENRY: Page 168, third paragraph, seventh line.

ROGGIE: ...Really?

HENRY: Yes.

ROGGIE: You're no fun.

HENRY: Yes I am. Under the proper circumstances.

(ROGGIE *gives the book back to* HENRY.)

HENRY: Joseph didn't respond when I told him I'd
want to go out on a date with him. It's customary to
respond to something like that. I would like to see him
so I can get a response to that question.

ROGGIE: You know I have a video about this on my channel. About what happens when a guy you like isn't at a party or whatever.

HENRY: Yes I remember. You say to focus on meeting other people because you never know who, or rather *whom*, you'll be missing.

ROGGIE: Exactly!

HENRY: I don't want to meet other people. Perhaps you can understand my feelings and permit me to stay in tonight.

ROGGIE: Okay, well say we go out, and Joseph is there, and you talk to him, and he ends up not wanting to go out on a date with you. Just, theoretically.

Know that I'll be here for you. Shoulder to cry on and all that. But you'll never know unless you come out.

HENRY: And even worse, he could not be there at all.

(ROGGIE's *cell phone dings. He looks at it.*)

ROGGIE: Our Lyft is here. Last call. Are you coming, or...?

HENRY: No.
(*He opens up his book and reads.*)

ROGGIE: Alright. But if you miss the love of your life tonight, don't blame me.

HENRY: I won't.

(ROGGIE *exits, leaving* HENRY *with his book.*)

Scene Five

(*January 2011. A dorm room.* KEN *is on his bed, anxious.* HENRY *looks at the books on* KEN's *shelf. A long moment.*)

KEN: Stare at my books long enough?

HENRY: No. I'm just judging you. I judge everyone by their books.

KEN: That the only thing?

HENRY: No, but it's the main one.

KEN: Yeah well…I didn't spend nearly as much time looking at your books last week.

HENRY: Give me a second please. I'm almost done.

KEN: You've been staring at them for like, five minutes.

(HENRY *looks at the bookshelf a bit longer. He then goes to* KEN *on the bed.*)

HENRY: You don't have any British books from the 19th century on your shelf.

KEN: Uh…no.

(KEN *kisses* HENRY. HENRY *doesn't respond.* KEN *tries to get* HENRY *to kiss him back. Instead,* HENRY *pulls away.*)

HENRY: Have you read any?

KEN: I'm an English major. Duh.

HENRY: What's your favorite?

KEN: Don't really have one. Not really into those books.

HENRY: Mine right now is *The Tenant of Wildfell Hall* by Anne Brontë. It used to be *The Woman in White* by Wilkie Collins.

KEN: Cool.

(KEN *tries to kiss* HENRY. HENRY *pulls away.*)

HENRY: Anne Brontë is not as well known as the other two because Charlotte hated her and her book. Actually, people think that *Jane Eyre* was the first book to talk about the governess plight in Victorian England, but actually—

KEN: Shut up and kiss me.

(KEN *kisses* HENRY. HENRY *pulls away.*)

HENRY: Anne wrote *Agnes Grey* first, which was pretty much the same plot, except it's not as long. Some people even think that Charlotte poisoned her sisters. I don't know if this is true, but either way, Charlotte didn't like Anne, and didn't think *Tenant of Wildfell Hall* was worth preserving. She literally wrote that the subject matter was a mistake.

KEN: Have you read anything that *wasn't* written in the Victorian era?

HENRY: Of course, Ken. I read everything my elementary, middle, and high schools assigned me to read.

KEN: I mean, on your own. Not for school.

HENRY: Yes.

KEN: Like what?

HENRY: Biograp hies of Victorian writers, mainly.

KEN: I mean other books written by authors who are still alive.

HENRY: No.

KEN: Really? Outside of school, you've *never* read a book by an author who wasn't living in the Victorian era?

HENRY: Well technically, Jane Austen is Regency, not Victorian...

KEN: I mean after 1900 or whatever.

HENRY: 1901. Queen Victoria died on January 22nd, 1901. Therefore, the Victorian era ended in 1901.

KEN: Okay. But I'm saying, there are *a lot* of other books out there. You're missing out. Andrew Holleran? Willa Cather? James Baldwin? Toni Morrison? Edmund White?

HENRY: I'm not interested in reading them.

KEN: So you'd rather read like *Wuthering Heights* for the umpteenth time—

HENRY: Sixty-eighth.

KEN: *Dude.* You need to *expand your horizons*! Let me just…

(KEN *goes to his bookshelf and pulls out a copy of* Maurice *by E M Forster and hands it to* HENRY.)

HENRY: *Maurice. (Pronounced moor-EEs).*

KEN: No, no. It's *Maurice. (Pronounced Morris)*

HENRY: I know this author. We read *Howards End* for my A P English class in high school. I didn't like it.

KEN: I think you'll like this one. E M Forster wrote it in like 1912 about a gay guy who was in love with a man, but it wasn't published until like a year after he died. It was illegal to be gay in England until 1967. Like, people could be executed for it. Or rather, *men* could be executed for it. Queen Victoria didn't believe that lesbians existed, so they were exempt from being executed. Which makes me wonder if Queen Victoria was possibly a lesbian herself—

HENRY: She was not. She and Albert were very much in love.

KEN: Sure. But it's possible for a woman in love with a guy to like other women, isn't it?

HENRY: It is. But not Queen Victoria.

KEN: Just a theory of mine.

HENRY: It's wrong.

KEN: *Anyway*, so E M Forster wrote that book, and he *really* wanted to give it a happy ending. But apparently the age-old rule that gay people have to be miserable and die at the end of their stories was in effect then, so he couldn't publish it.

HENRY: Oscar Wilde was gay, too.

KEN: Yeah, and he was put on trial for it.

HENRY: 1895.

KEN: Yeah. And that happened less than twenty years before *Maurice* was written. Anyway, it's really interesting. If you want to borrow it, go for it.

(HENRY *considers the book.*)

HENRY: No thank you. I already know that being gay was horrible back then. I don't need to be reminded of it.

KEN: But...don't you want to know about your history? As a gay man, I mean?

HENRY: You spoke about how gay men were executed under Queen Victoria's rule. I've known that for a long time. I do not need to be reminded of it.

KEN: But...you don't want to engage with the art of other gay men?

HENRY: Just because I'm gay does not mean I am required to only like gay things.
Oscar Wilde, for example, wrote hilarious comedies-of-manners. His homosexuality does not impact what I think of his writing.

KEN: So you don't think *Oscar Wilde* being gay had *anything* to do with his writing?

HENRY: No.

KEN: Okay, *that's* a long discussion I'm not willing to have right now...

HENRY: Me neither.

(KEN *takes* Maurice *from* HENRY *and places it on the shelf. He searches the shelf for another book.*)

KEN: Then why don't I find you something else that—
Oh! There's this really good memoir that—

HENRY: I don't read memoir.

(KEN *pulls out a book and hands it to* HENRY.)

KEN: You *have to* at least give this book a shot.
Seriously, it blew my mind in terms of what literature
can do, or should be—

HENRY: *Should* be?

KEN: Yeah.

HENRY: Literature just needs to tell a good story
that discusses the society it's in and speaks to other
societies in the future. That's all that literature needs to
do.

KEN: And you think it can't do anything else? Like
bring about social change?

HENRY: It can bring about awareness, yes. Charles
Dickens did that all the time.

KEN: Oh my God, I HATE Dickens! We had to read
A Tale of Two Cities in high school. *Why* teach that
anymore!? Too many subplots, too many characters—

HENRY: That's actually my favorite of his.

KEN: Sorry, but you gotta admit, it's *a lot.*

HENRY: I was able to comprehend it. You were not.
And that's okay. You don't have to comprehend
everything.

KEN: Wow. That's like...
You're impossible. You know that? This whole night,
you've just been really...

HENRY: Really...?
Please finish your sentence.

KEN: I'm going to do the *nice* thing and not finish it. You're not going to read that book, are you?

HENRY: I said I wasn't interested.

KEN: Not interested in *anything* outside of the 19th century Anglo-Saxon milieu. Duly noted.

(KEN *sighs and takes his book back from* HENRY *and replaces it on the shelf.* HENRY *then pulls out a copy of* Wuthering Heights *from his pocket.)*

HENRY: So I don't suppose you would want this then.

KEN: *Wuthering Heights*!? Are you *for real*!?

HENRY: It's one of the most romantic books I've ever read. I figured we could possibly—

KEN: I can't believe—
You *really* thought I was going to want to read that after rejecting *every* book I recommend to you?

HENRY: It's a classic.

KEN: I read it in high school. It sucked. Now get the hell out of here.

(HENRY *puts the book back in his pocket and exits.)*

Scene Six

(*The cabin in Upstate New York. August 2017. Later that night.* HENRY *is lying in his bed. We can't tell if he's sleeping. The door opens.* ROGGIE, *very drunk, is being ushered in by* JOSEPH.)

ROGGIE: That…that frickin' asshole, had no right to…

JOSEPH: No he didn't.

ROGGIE: Like, he calls *me* a stalker!? He's been at *every party* I've been to this weekend! What does that say about him!? Doesn't he realize it's just *coincidence*!?

JOSEPH: You need water. Can I turn on the lights?

ROGGIE: WE SHOULDN'T WAKE—
(Whispers)
We shouldn't wake up Henry.

HENRY: I'm already up.

ROGGIE: *Shiiiiiiiiiit!*

(JOSEPH turns on the light. HENRY sees him and immediately gets out of bed and stands before him. He holds his hand out.)

HENRY: Hello again, Joseph.

(JOSEPH shakes HENRY's hand.)

JOSEPH: You remembered my name.

HENRY: Yes. I have a great facility for names and faces.

ROGGIE: I blame *you* for tonight, Henry.

(JOSEPH finds a bottle of water and gives it to ROGGIE.)

ROGGIE: You made me go out *alone* to face my *asshole* of an ex. *Alone.* And not just *any* ex of mine. *Jackson.*

JOSEPH: Drink.

(ROGGIE opens the bottled water and drinks.)

ROGGIE: But look who was also there! Didn't I tell you you never knew he would be there if you didn't come out with me? And now he's here! He was kind enough to take me home.

JOSEPH: Drink your water.

(ROGGIE drinks his water. He flings himself backwards on his bed.)

ROGGIE: So Jackson was all like, "You're stalking me!" And I'm like, "No, I'm here to have a good time like you, *you're* the one who cheated on me…" And he was like, "Maybe if you weren't such a *slut* I wouldn't have."

And then I'm like, "*You* slept with a *girl* behind my back. Doesn't that make *you* the slut?"

JOSEPH: Water. Drink.

(ROGGIE *drinks. He drinks sporadically throughout the next monologue.*)

ROGGIE: And he's like, "It's not cheating if it's a girl." And I'm like, *really* pissed off at this point, "If it's another hole, it's cheating."
And like, I can't believe I actually *loved* this guy . Like, I really *loved* this guy . But now he's just like, calling me a stalker, even though we've been on and off since fucking *college*, and now he's telling everyone I'm a stalker, and I'm not, and I'm just like, I'm getting with other people, like *he* did, and it's been *great* to feel like, *free*. To just like, get with other people, whenever I want, and not have to feel guilty about it, like, you know…

(ROGGIE *drinks.* HENRY *takes out a copy of* Jane Eyre.)

(ROGGIE *sees this.*)

ROGGIE: Awwww, you're going to read to me? How sweet, Henry. You're so sweet…

(HENRY *opens the book.*)

HENRY: "And if I had loved him less I should have thought his accent and look of exultation savage; but, sitting by him, roused from the nightmare of parting—called to the paradise of union—I thought only of the bliss given me to drink in so abundant a flow."

(ROGGIE *begins to drift off.*)

ROGGIE: I love it when you read to me, Henry. Don't stop reading to me… Don't stop…

HENRY: "Again and again he said, 'Are you happy, Jane?' And again and again I answered, 'Yes.' After which he murmured, 'It will atone—it will atone.'"

(ROGGIE *starts snoring.* HENRY *closes the book and puts it away.*)

JOSEPH: Do you do that every time he comes in drunk?

HENRY: If I'm not asleep, which I'm usually not, yes.

JOSEPH: That's...sweet.

HENRY: Roggie and I have been roommates since junior year of college.

JOSEPH: Yeah?

HENRY: Yes. My roommate junior year decided he didn't want to room with an Aspie, and Roggie's roommate was really homophobic. So we met at a roommate mixer on our campus and next thing I knew he was my roommate.

JOSEPH: Aspie?

HENRY: Asperger's Syndrome. I'm autistic.

JOSEPH: Oh okay. Actually, I figured, but I didn't wanna say anything.

HENRY: Yes. Diagnosed at age four when I wasn't speaking as early as other children.

JOSEPH: I see. So you and Roggie still live together?

HENRY: Yes. He moved to New York for work, I was moving to New York for graduate school, and we decided to get an apartment together. It's worked for the most part.
He brings home a lot of guys, but I don't mind. He once said, when he was quite drunk, that if I wasn't his roommate, he would ask me out.

JOSEPH: Did you two ever...?

HENRY: Ever...? Please finish your sentence.

JOSEPH: Go out? Or...have sex?

HENRY: Neither. There was a time I wanted to. But we concurred that it would make our cohabitation too awkward.

JOSEPH: You ever watch his YouTube channel, or...?

HENRY: Yes. I've seen every episode because Roggie asked me to, but I don't care about them. They're for people who have sex lives. I don't have a sex life. I'm not interested in sex. Usually. I'm not *usually* interested in sex.

JOSEPH: I see...

HENRY: You seem like a person who has sex a lot.

(JOSEPH *chuckles.*)

JOSEPH: Why do you say that?

HENRY: Roggie told me you liked to play the field, so I figure you must have a lot of sex.

JOSEPH: Did he now?

HENRY: Yes.

JOSEPH: Well...I don't, actually. I used to in college, but...
Now I only have sex with people I really connect with. You know?

HENRY: Me too.

(*Pause.* HENRY *and* JOSEPH *look at each other. Tension mounting*)

JOSEPH: My brother's autistic, actually.
But like, he can't speak, or take care of himself, my parents have to make sure they have 24/7 care for him.

HENRY: Sounds severe.

JOSEPH: Yeah. We love him, but it gets frustrating with him sometimes. My parents still describe him as "mentally retarded", which is like, not something you should describe *anyone* as. He still deserves everything "normal" people tend to get. Love, affection. Like, to say he's "mentally r-worded" is just so dismissive to me.

HENRY: I was called that a lot too, growing up. By my enemies and people I thought were not my enemies. It hurt more when the people I thought were not my enemies said it, because then I had to wonder if they thought that for the whole of our acquaintance. But I was glad to know that they were false friends.

JOSEPH: Yeah…

HENRY: What is your brother's name?

JOSEPH: Ian.

HENRY: Is he older or younger?

JOSEPH: Younger. By two years.

HENRY: Do you ever wish he was normal?

JOSEPH: What kind of a question is that?

HENRY: My mother wishes I were normal. She wishes I adhered to "social cues" more. But as the old saying goes, I believe in marching to the beat of my own drum.

JOSEPH: Cool.
Can I ask…what's it like? To be…to have Asperger's? Or like, autism in general?

HENRY: It feels like…
Sometimes. I feel like there's a light switch inside of me. Like when I think of Jane Austen. Or the Brontë sisters. Or Charles Dickens. And it's always flipped upwards for those subjects and people. And it's a big light switch, so it takes up a lot of space. But it's hard to turn it off, because when it gets turned off, there's nothing.

I talk to other people, or see other people talking,
and I can tell that they all have light switches, too. Of
varying sizes. And they have the ability to flip these
switches on and off, flip multiple switches at once. And
they rarely go dark because if there's one light switch
off, they can always turn on another. There's never
darkness, nor nothingness in them. Whereas with me, I
only have the one.

But when I *can* turn my switch on, I can engage with
people again. Until I have to turn it off again.

Sometimes, I'd give anything to have access to every
light switch possible.

(He picks up Jane Eyre.*)*

But then. I think about what these authors have given
us... Stories that still reach out and resonate, even
from a time when people like me would have been
imprisoned, or executed, or put in an insane asylum.
Stories that still have *something to say.* And you *really
want* people to listen to what they have to say.

And you get so so so *exasperated and flabbergasted* when
they don't, you just can't help but want to *scream*,
LISTEN, DAMMIT. LISTEN.

JOSEPH: Ssshhh...

*(*ROGGIE *stirs in his bed. Doesn't wake up)*

HENRY: I apologize. Does that answer your question?

JOSEPH: Yeah.

You're very passionate. I like that about you.

(A moment as HENRY *and* JOSEPH *hold each other's gaze.)*

HENRY: Can you touch me again? Anywhere. Even my
waist.

(Silence. A long, long, moment. JOSEPH *touches* HENRY *on
the chest, the waist. The two then lean into each other. They
kiss. When they part,* HENRY *leads* JOSEPH *to his bed, where
they continue kissing.)*

JOSEPH: Wait. Roggie.

HENRY: He's passed out. And he sleeps like a hibernating bear. And he'll be happy that I'm with a guy.

JOSEPH: If you say so…

(JOSEPH *goes in to kiss* HENRY. HENRY *pulls away.*)

HENRY: Wait! Before I forget.

(HENRY *digs in his bag and pulls out a copy of* Wuthering Heights. *He hands it to* JOSEPH.)

JOSEPH: *Wuthering Heights.*

HENRY: It's by Emily Brontë. The sister of Charlotte Brontë, who wrote *Jane Eyre.* This one is much darker, and the characters are much meaner, but it's beautiful. I used to play a game based off this book back when I was in fifth grade. But I was the only one who liked the game. It's the most romantic book because it's so violently passionate. It shows that love can't be love if it's compromised. And that's what I believe. And I want you to read it.

JOSEPH: Thanks, but…I couldn't take your copy of it.

HENRY: Oh I have eighteen others. It's okay.

JOSEPH: Eighteen?

HENRY: And counting.
When was the last time you read a book?

JOSEPH: For pleasure? I don't know, like…senior year of college? It was about an autistic kid, and it involved a dog, or…?

HENRY: *The Curious Incident of the Dog in the Night-Time.*

JOSEPH: You've read it?

HENRY: No. But my mother has and she wouldn't shut up about it for a time. She wanted me to read it, but I had scheduled myself to read all of Thomas Hardy's books.

JOSEPH: It's really good. You should read it. Maybe it'll flip another light switch in you.

HENRY: And maybe reading *this* will flip a light switch in *you*.

(JOSEPH *takes the book, looks at it. He puts it on the floor.*)

JOSEPH: Possibly.
But right now, in this second, I'm more interested in… (*He kisses* HENRY. *He then goes to the light switch in the cabin.*)

HENRY: In…? Please finish your sentence.

(JOSEPH *grins at* HENRY, *and turns the light out.*)

Scene Seven

(*August 2005. A restaurant.* HENRY *and* MARIAN. HENRY *is reading* Jude the Obscure. *Awkwardness*)

MARIAN: Did I tell you about the actor on that show I watch?

(*A moment.* HENRY *then closes his book, marking his page.*)

HENRY: I apologize, Mama (*Pronounced muh-MAH*). I wanted to complete this chapter. What did you just say?

MARIAN: This actor on that show I watch. They were interviewing him and he said he was—

HENRY: If this is about those trashy soap operas you consume, I am not interested.

(*He opens* Jude the Obscure *to where he left off.*)

MARIAN: He's autistic, too.
(*She squints, trying to read the title of the book* HENRY *is reading.*)

"Jude the…

HENRY: "Obscure."

MARIAN: I remember that book. I read it in college. Thomas Hardy, right?

HENRY: Yes.

MARIAN: Okay. Or was it something else by Thomas Hardy that I read? What else did he write?

(HENRY *puts down his book, perhaps a bit too eagerly.*)

HENRY: *A Pair of Blue Eyes, Tess of the d'Urbervilles, The Mayor of Casterbridge, The Return of the Native*—

MARIAN: Maybe it was that one.

HENRY: I wasn't done yet. *The Woodlanders, Far from the Madding Crowd* which is my least favorite book of his—

MARIAN: Henry—

HENRY: *Desperate Remedies, Under the Greenwood Tree,* his first novel was actually going to be called *The Poor Man and the Lady* but his friends thought it would be too politically controversial so he burned the manuscript—

MARIAN: Henry!

HENRY: I'm almost done, Mama.
He also wrote a lot of poetry. I've read all his poems. I like his novels better, but that's because I find novels much more to my interest.
Two on a Tower and *The Well-Beloved.*

MARIAN: HENRY!

HENRY: I'm done, Mama.

MARIAN: I asked you to stop three times, and you kept going.

HENRY: I wanted to finish.

MARIAN: Did I ask you to finish?

HENRY: No, but—

MARIAN: Could you tell I wanted to say something?

HENRY: You were saying my name.

MARIAN: And you kept cutting me off. *Social cues,*
Henry. When someone wants to say something, you
let them say it. Didn't your social skills group go over
this?

HENRY: Yes they did, Mama.

MARIAN: Then you should have *learned this by now.* For
God's sake, Henry. You're fifteen!

HENRY: I know, Mama…

MARIAN: And why do you call me Mama? Just call me
mom. Or at least Mother.

HENRY: Why should I not call you Mama? It's a way
people address the women who bore them. I mean give
birth. Not induce boredom.

MARIAN: And what's with this weird way of speaking
you have? "Why should I not" and "much more to my
interest."

HENRY: That was how people talked in these books,
Mama.

MARIAN: Those books were written in the 1800s,
Henry. We're not living in the 1800s.

HENRY: I know. But just because I'm a part of a society
doesn't mean I have to speak like them. I find a
dreadful lack of eloquence in much of today's verbiage.

MARIAN: You have to talk at other people's levels.
Otherwise, you're not gonna have any friends.

HENRY: I care not about having friends.

MARIAN: What about when you start dating girls?

HENRY: Who said I will be dating girls, Mama?

MARIAN: *(Joking)* Oh, do you mean you're gay?

(Pause. HENRY chooses his words very carefully—more carefully than before.)

MARIAN: Henry… Are you…?

HENRY: I've pondered and pondered how I wanted to tell you. And I had hoped that the topic would be broached in a more private environment. But I see that I will have to press on with what I have to say.
Mama.
Mom.
I am pretty sure I am a homosexual.

(Long pause as MARIAN takes this in.)

HENRY: Are you mad with me, Mama?

MARIAN: No, Henry. No, I'm not mad…
You know you… You could've just said, "Yes I'm gay," right?

HENRY: No. "Gay" means you're happy. "Homosexual" means you have romantic proclivities towards the same gender. They're hardly the same thing.

(A moment. Then, MARIAN begins to cry softly. HENRY takes out a handkerchief he has been keeping in his pocket and hands it to MARIAN.)

HENRY: Why are you crying, Mama?

MARIAN: It's just…I always knew life was going to be so, so hard for you. And now it's only going to be harder for you.
I only ever wanted things to be easy for you, Henry. But now, with this, being…

HENRY: Homosexual. It's only a word.

MARIAN: Homosexual. I just worry, Henry. About how things are going to be for you.

HENRY: Don't worry about me mama. One day I will find a nice man who will keep me safe and happy for the remainder of my days.

MARIAN: I hope so, Henry. I really hope so.

HENRY: Or at least, will do something so kind, so generous for me, that I can't help but fall in love with him. Like how Elizabeth falls in love with Darcy after he helps Lydia and Mr Wickham. I used to think it was just after she saw his house, but I reread the book recently, and she *actually* realizes she loves him after she sees he can be incredibly nice not just to her, but also to her family, whom he barely tolerates at first.

(MARIAN *laughs.*)

HENRY: What? What is it, Mama?

MARIAN: I love you, Henry. And I really hope you find someone who loves you as much as you deserve to be loved.

HENRY: And who will find me most tolerable.

MARIAN: I want someone to feel more than just tolerance for you.

HENRY: Perhaps one day they will. Now I'm going to go back to my book.

(HENRY *reopens* Jude the Obscure *and keeps reading.* MARIAN *looks at him.*)

Scene Eight

(*August 2017. The cabin in Upstate New York. The morning after Scene Six.* JOSEPH *has left.* HENRY *wakes up. He looks at the floor, to where* JOSEPH *had dropped the copy of* Wuthering Heights. *The book is gone. In its place is a note.* HENRY *picks up the note and reads it. He smiles and jumps out of bed and goes to* ROGGIE, *who is still asleep.*)

HENRY: Roggie!!! Roggie Roggie Roggie!!!

(ROGGIE *stirs.*)

ROGGIE: What the fuck, Henry...

HENRY: Look!!!
(*He waves the note in* ROGGIE'*s face.*)

ROGGIE: Get that out of my face.

HENRY: It's a note. From Joseph.

ROGGIE: Oh...

HENRY: He slept over last night.

ROGGIE: Did he now.

HENRY: He and I also had sex. Which I knew would make you happy. He let me inside him. We were quiet because we didn't want to wake you up.

ROGGIE: Thanks for being considerate?

HENRY: I told him I wanted to lend him my copy of *Wuthering Heights*, and he seemed like he wasn't going to take it, but then I woke up, and I found the book gone, and I found this note, and it says that he'll give the book a chance, and he left his number!!!

ROGGIE: How...retro? I dunno.

HENRY: I'll have to call him.

ROGGIE: You could text him, too.

HENRY: No, I'd like to call him. It's more personal that way.

ROGGIE: Whatever floats your boat.

(HENRY *takes his phone and calls* JOSEPH.)

HENRY: Hi Joseph. It's Henry. I'm calling you because you left your number in a note last night. I wanted to call you so that you had my number. Have you started *Wuthering Heights* yet? Let me know when you've

started the book so we can talk about it. Whenever
I read it, it usually takes me about three days. One
hundred pages per day. Sometimes I can get it done
in two. The parts where Joseph speaks you might
want to slow down a bit. He speaks with a really thick
Yorkshire accent, and Emily Brontë writes it that way,
so you might have to translate it in your head to get
it. Or you can just call me and I can translate it for
you. Either way, I can't wait for you to read it and tell
me what you think. Thank you for leaving me your
number. I can't wait to talk to you again. Bye.
(He hangs up.)
It went to voicemail.

ROGGIE: I figured.

HENRY: Do you think he'll call me back?

ROGGIE: He'll probably text you back, more likely.

(ROGGIE *finds his water bottle and drinks from it.* HENRY
sits on his bed and looks at his phone.)

ROGGIE: You're looking at your phone.

HENRY: I'm waiting for a message from Joseph.

ROGGIE: You mean, you're *not* going to read a book?
You're going to *look at your phone* instead? Look at you,
becoming a millennial.

HENRY: I *am* a millennial. I was born in 1990—

ROGGIE: It was a *joke,* Henry. Just a *joke.*

HENRY: Well it wasn't very funny.

ROGGIE: Sorry…

HENRY: You said he wasn't really the kind of person
who dated, Roggie. But maybe, he is. We talked about
a lot of personal things last night. Like about his
brother. Who is also autistic. Did you know that about
him?

ROGGIE: No.

HENRY: And he took my book when he could have just left it behind. Perhaps that means he'll want to talk to me again when he's done reading it. And when we talk, we'll want to talk more, and see each other more, and then—

ROGGIE: What if he doesn't give it back?

HENRY: He will. He must. It's only proper that he does.

ROGGIE: Henry, stop and think for a—

HENRY: What good can thinking do me now!? Please, Roggie. *Please* let me have this. I've never...*felt* anything like this. Like, the possibility that something could actually *happen*.

ROGGIE: Alright. Whatever. But, if this goes wrong for any reason—

HENRY: I won't need your shoulder to cry on. I won't need it for a long time. Because for once...

Ask me if I'm happy.

ROGGIE: Are you happy.

HENRY: Yes. Yes. Yes. Yes. Yes. Yes. Yes. Yes. Yes. Yes. Yes. Yes.Yes. Yes. Yes. Yes. Yes.Yes!!!

(With every "Yes", the lights grow brighter and brighter. We hear switches being flipped upwards. HENRY beams at the audience. ROGGIE looks at him, concerned. Once the lights have reached their maxim...)

(Blackout)

END OF ACT ONE

ACT TWO

Scene Nine

(A dorm room. February 2011. HENRY *is at his desk typing a paper. He has a copy of* Jane Eyre *next to him. The door opens and* ROGGIE *enters, rather wasted.)*

ROGGIE: Happy Valentine's Day!!!

HENRY: Valentine's Day isn't until tomorrow.

ROGGIE: It's like, one A M on the 13th, so it's *basically* Valentine's Day.

HENRY: But it isn't actually Valentine's Day. Valentine's Day is on the 14th, and it is not the 14th.

ROGGIE: Well aren't *you* soooooo correeeect...

*(*ROGGIE *stumbles on the way to his bed.* HENRY *gets up and steadies him.)*

ROGGIE: Thank you.

*(*HENRY *sets* ROGGIE *on his bed.* HENRY *then gets* ROGGIE *a bottle of water, opens it, and gives it to him.)*

ROGGIE: Thank you very much.
(He sips water.)
You know like, one of the reasons I *love* being your roommate is that whenever I come back to the dorm wasted off my ass, you're like *always* there to like, help me get to bed. You're like, one of the few gay guys

on campus who's actually *decent*. Like, Voldemort
tonight...I mean Jackson...Voldemort is the villain
from *Harry Potter*—

HENRY: I know who Voldemort is.
I may not have read the books, but I know who he is.

ROGGIE: So like, Jackson texted me that he loved me
yesterday. And then at the party tonight, he like, *totally*
ditched me for this girl. He says she's his best friend,
but there's *totally* something going on between them.
Like, I get that he isn't *out*, and if he's bi than like great,
whatever, but don't like, take advantage of it. Or other
people.

HENRY: Why do you still see him if he makes you think
of Voldemort?

ROGGIE: Because when we *are* together, it's like,
amazing. Like, Henry, imagine what you and Ken had
and multiply that by like, ten billion, and that's what
Jackson and I have.

HENRY: Ken wasn't very nice to me.

ROGGIE: He was so *mean* because he wanted you to
read books that weren't Victorian! The *horror*!

HENRY: You deserve someone who is at least nice to
you, Roggie.

ROGGIE: I know. But I like mean people so *much better*.
Don't you? I don't wanna like mean people...

HENRY: Ken and I only had sex once. It was a lovely
encounter. But he didn't appreciate what I had to offer.

ROGGIE: Henry.

HENRY: Yes, Roggie.

ROGGIE: Henry Henry Henry.

HENRY: Roggie Roggie Roggie.

ROGGIE: Can you read to me?

HENRY: Of course. Anything in particular?

ROGGIE: You pick. As long as it's not scary. I don't like scary bedtime stories.

HENRY: So *Frankenstein* is out. Duly noted.

(ROGGIE laughs.)

ROGGIE: I don't know why...I find that so funny.

HENRY: How's about...

(He goes to his desk to get his copy of Jane Eyre. *He opens it to a page.)*

"And if I had loved him less I should have thought his accent and look of exultation savage; but, sitting by him, roused from the nightmare of parting—called to the paradise of union—I thought only of the bliss given me to drink in so abundant a flow. Again and again he said, 'Are you happy, Jane?' And again and again I answered, 'Yes.' After which he murmured, 'It will atone—it will atone.'"

ROGGIE: Every time you read to me...I never know what it means. But it's so nice.

HENRY: It's from *Jane Eyre*. They're some of the most passionate words ever written in the English language.

ROGGIE: If only I knew what they meant. Then maybe I'd understand real passion...Henry?

HENRY: Yes Roggie.

ROGGIE: I would *totally* ask you out if you weren't like...

(A long pause)

HENRY: If I wasn't like...? Please finish your sentence.

(Pause)

ROGGIE: If you weren't like...my roommate. I'd totally ask you out.

HENRY: Why?

ROGGIE: You're like, smart. And you know what you want to do. I have no idea what I want to do. And it like sucks, because in college you're supposed to know what you want to do, and I don't...

HENRY: You want to sleep with men. You do plenty of that. Certainly more than I.

ROGGIE: I wanna do more than *that*, Henry, I wanna like...*help* people. But I don't know how.

HENRY: You could be a gay male sex therapist. You know a lot about gay male sex.

ROGGIE: You know, I *have* thought about starting my own vlog. Or something. I don't know, though... Maybe *you* should start a vlog too! About like... Victorian stuff, or...

HENRY: Would you watch it?

ROGGIE: Sure. Why not. I read *Wuthering Heights,* right? But like I was saying, yeah, I wouldn't wanna mess the whole roommate thing up... You understand, right...?

HENRY: Yes I do.

(Pause)

Roggie?

(ROGGIE doesn't respond. He falls asleep. HENRY takes ROGGIE's bedsheets and covers him with them. He then returns to his desk and continues writing his paper.)

Scene Ten

(September 2017. HENRY and ROGGIE's apartment living room. HENRY leaving a voice mail.)

HENRY: Hi Joseph. It's Henry. This is the fifteenth voice message I have left you in the past month. I just

wanted to check in and see how you were doing on
Wuthering Heights. I can't wait to talk to you about it.
I also can't wait to talk to you in general. I had a very
good time in bed with you and I hope we can repeat
that.

(Pause as he figures out what to say next.)

I said in my voice message two days ago that some
people don't like it because all of the characters
were unlikable. They're not all unlikeable. Nellie is
alright, she just finds herself in a tough situation with
Catherine.

(ROGGIE enters and listens.)

HENRY: And there are a few other characters whom I
don't want to name yet because I don't want to spoil
the book for you, but they're likable.

Also I left you a voicemail reading all of Joseph's parts.
Those are some of the sections

that people have the most difficulty getting through,
so I wanted to make it as easy for you as possible. I
also figured it would be a nice thing to do. So you're
welcome, in advance.

Until we speak again. Good bye.

*(He puts down the phone, considers putting it back to his
ear, then ends up turning it off. He turns around and sees
ROGGIE.)*

I don't believe he's read the book. What could be
taking him so long?

ROGGIE: He could be a slow reader? He also could have
forgotten about it? There could be a lot of reasons.
And just saying, you've also been texting and calling
him *a lot*.

HENRY: How else can I assure he'll get back to me?

ROGGIE: You've seen my video about this, right? If you're constantly calling and texting a guy you hook up with and he's not getting back to you—

HENRY: We didn't hook up. We had sex. There's a difference.

ROGGIE: Okay. But if a guy I just slept with was constantly calling me to ask about a book I frankly had no interest in reading—

HENRY: He *wanted* to read it. I know because he *took the book*. And if you take someone's book, you read it, and give it back. And if someone contacts you, you get back to them. That's how it goes!!!

ROGGIE: Not always. Sometimes people forget to give things back, or get back to people. I forget things all the time. It's not a big deal.

HENRY: It should be a big deal. It's incredibly poor manners. If Jane Austen were alive, she would look down upon you most condescendingly.

ROGGIE: I'm letting that slide because I know you're upset. But what Joseph's doing isn't exactly a crime. And besides, you have nineteen copies of that book.

HENRY: Eighteen now!

ROGGIE: That's still seventeen more than the average person has.

HENRY: It's still *my copy*!

ROGGIE: I know it's a big deal to you, but Joseph will get back to you when—

HENRY: It's been a month. It takes me one *week* at the *absolute most* to read *Wuthering Heights*.

ROGGIE: Not everyone reads like you do.

HENRY: Well they should. Then maybe I wouldn't be kept waiting for so long.

(He takes out his phone and taps on the screen.)
Maybe I should call him again and tell him how angry
I'm—

(ROGGIE takes HENRY's phone from him.)

ROGGIE: Noooo nonono. You are *not* calling him again.
(He taps on HENRY's phone.)

HENRY: What are you doing!?

ROGGIE: Deleting his number.

HENRY: 212 555-3904.

*(ROGGIE looks down at the phone. HENRY is right. He hands
it back.)*

ROGGIE: If *anything*, can you at least *try* not to call him?
For at least a week. For all you know, he might call you
back in that time!

HENRY: What if he doesn't?

ROGGIE: Then he doesn't. But honestly, what you're
doing now… It's probably making him *not* want to talk
to you.
(Pause)
Hey.

*(ROGGIE opens his arms. HENRY doesn't go in for a hug.
Instead…)*

HENRY: I'm giving him as much room as I feel
necessary. Contrary to what you think, I actually know
what I'm doing in this situation. So kindly keep your
unsolicited censuring to *yourself.*

(ROGGIE holds up his hands.)

ROGGIE: Alright.

*(ROGGIE exits. HENRY looks at his phone. He taps on it,
then looks at it. He keeps looking at it.)*

HENRY: Do not keep me waiting, Joseph. Please do not keep me waiting. Please do not make a Miss Havisham of me.

Scene Eleven

(The summer house in Upstate New York. The library. A few days after the previous scene. JOSEPH and ANOTHER GUY are making out.)

ANOTHER GUY: I thought this room was off-limits to hookups.

JOSEPH: It is. But you're an exception to the rule.

ANOTHER GUY: I feel so special.

JOSEPH: That's because you are.

(JOSEPH and ANOTHER GUY continue making out. Just then, someone tries to open the door. It is locked.)

JOSEPH: They'll leave in a second.

(Whomever is behind the door keeps trying to get in.)

(There is knocking. JOSEPH rolls his eyes and gets up.)

JOSEPH: Hold on.

(JOSEPH goes to the door and opens it. ROGGIE stands behind it.)

JOSEPH: This room is occupied at the moment.

ROGGIE: I've been looking for you.

JOSEPH: Can it wait?

ROGGIE: No.

ANOTHER GUY: I can go if…

JOSEPH: No, stay right—

ROGGIE: Yeah. You're gonna wanna go.

(ANOTHER GUY *raises his hands and leaves the room, leaving* ROGGIE *and* JOSEPH *alone.*)

JOSEPH: What is it, Roggie?

ROGGIE: It's Henry.

JOSEPH: Oh my God. Can you tell him to *stop calling me?* Seriously, it's been *non-stop* since I took that book of his.

ROGGIE: Yeah, I know.

JOSEPH: Have you *heard* some of the messages he sent me??? Some of them go on for *at least* half an hour.

ROGGIE: I can imagine.

JOSEPH: No, he spent an *entire voicemail* reading passages from *Wuthering Heights* saying that he was translating one of the characters or something?

ROGGIE: Joseph. The character, I mean. He has a really thick Yorkshire accent that Henry figured might be difficult for you to—

JOSEPH: Oh God, he's not *here* with you, is he?

ROGGIE: No. He's back in the city.

JOSEPH: Did he send you himself?

ROGGIE: No. He doesn't know I'm here, actually.

JOSEPH: So what, are you trying to guilt me into—

ROGGIE: It's been a month, Joseph.

JOSEPH: A month without some stupid book that he has like, a million copies of.

ROGGIE: Nineteen. Eighteen, technically.
And it's not just about the book.

JOSEPH: What, does he think I'm in love with him or something?

(ROGGIE *gives* JOSEPH *a knowing look.*)

JOSEPH: Oh God...

ROGGIE: You took the book. That meant something to him.

JOSEPH: I can give it back. Here, I'll give it back to you right—

ROGGIE: He expects you to have *read* it.

JOSEPH: Well...tell him I did, I liked it, I didn't want to talk about it, stop blowing up my phone. Okay?

ROGGIE: You can't do that with Henry. I know he's a bit socially retarded, but—

JOSEPH: Wait, are you saying he's retarded because he's autistic? My brother's autistic too. It doesn't make him retarded.

ROGGIE: ...You're right. Sorry.

JOSEPH: So I really don't appreciate you using that word.

ROGGIE: I meant it more like, Henry just really loves this stuff, and wants other people to love it. And honestly, *Wuthering Heights* is a pretty good book.

JOSEPH: Did he force you to read it too?

ROGGIE: I mean yeah. But...I ended up not minding. I mean I didn't end up *loving* it, like Henry does, *no one* can love them like he does, which is something I really admire about him, actually, but...I liked it.
Look, just call him, tell him that you plan to read it, read the damn thing, meet up with him—

JOSEPH: Like, in person?

ROGGIE: Yes, in person.
Talk to him about it, then you'll be done with him.

JOSEPH: What does it mean to you?

ROGGIE: Nothing. Just…I don't want Henry to get hurt. He's really like…

JOSEPH: Clingy ?

ROGGIE: No. More like…he has certain expectations of people. And when they don't fulfill those expectations, he gets a little…edgy, you know? Maybe it's the Asperger's. I don't know. Either way, I've told him to not expect you to become his boyfriend. Multiple times.
But I *do* think you should give the book a chance, at least.
I did a video about this, actually. About giving people chances. And how that can lead to the best relationships that aren't necessarily romantic.
And how people can surprise you… You never know.

JOSEPH: You've grown accustomed to his idiosyncrasies, haven't you.

ROGGIE: Yeah. I guess you can say I have. And maybe…you will, too.

(JOSEPH *considers.*)

JOSEPH: If I knew I would have to read a book after having sex with him, I wouldn't have done it.

ROGGIE: I've been asked to shit on someone after having sex with them, so having to read *Wuthering Heights* after sex isn't the worst thing.
You said your brother was autistic, right? What if someone was doing to him what you're doing to Henry?

JOSEPH: I wouldn't call him "socially R-worded", for one thing.

ROGGIE: But you wouldn't want your brother to be led on. Or hurt by someone he liked. Right?

JOSEPH: No. I wouldn't.

ROGGIE: So…?

JOSEPH: Okay. Fine. I'll read it. I'll meet up with him.
But you seriously owe me one.

ROGGIE: Thank you.
(He opens the door and calls out.)
You may proceed.

*(ANOTHER GUY enters as ROGGIE leaves [the same guy as
before, lest there be any confusion].)*

ANOTHER GUY: What was that about?

JOSEPH: Nothing.

ANOTHER GUY: Is he like, the hookup who won't go
away or something?

JOSEPH: Kinda…
Hey, um. Random question. Have you read *Wuthering
Heights*?

ANOTHER GUY: Total secret?

JOSEPH: Yeah?

ANOTHER GUY: It's actually my favorite book.

JOSEPH: Really?

ANOTHER GUY: Yeah. But like, I don't tell anyone,
unless someone else brings it up, because no one reads
that Victorian crap. But like, I love it. It speaks to like,
the dark part of my soul.

JOSEPH: I'm thinking of reading it.

ANOTHER GUY: You totally should. And then we can
talk about it. Like a book club!

JOSEPH: Yeah. We can do that. But first…

(JOSEPH and ANOTHER GUY make out as the lights dim.)

Scene Twelve

(October, 2017. A café. HENRY *waits at a table. On the table are two cups and another one of his copies of* Wuthering Heights. *He stims by tapping his wrist with a pen. He checks his cell phone, worried.)*

*(*JOSEPH *enters. A look of relief washes over* HENRY.*)*

JOSEPH: Hey. Sorry I'm late.

HENRY: You're only two minutes late. That's not very late at all.

JOSEPH: Okay, good.
(He takes his coffee cup.)
Thanks for the coffee.

HENRY: You're welcome.
It's good to see you Joseph.

JOSEPH: You too.

HENRY: I was very glad when you called me back. I feared my messages weren't going through.

JOSEPH: No, they definitely were.

(Pause)

HENRY: So you read *Wuthering Heights.*

*(*JOSEPH *takes out the copy of* Wuthering Heights *and puts it on the table.)*

JOSEPH: I did!

HENRY: And...?

JOSEPH: *(Sincerely)* I...really enjoyed it. A lot, actually.

HENRY: Good!

JOSEPH: Yeah! I feel bad that it took me almost a month to read it. I mean it took a little while for me to really get into, since we, I mean *most* of us, don't really talk like that anymore. So the language took some adjusting.

HENRY: Understandable.

JOSEPH: But once I got into it, I was really…I mean the atmosphere alone is like…

HENRY: Stormy. Dangerous.

JOSEPH: Yeah. Very…dark, you know?

HENRY: It's a great demonstration of pathetic fallacy, which is when the weather reflects the actions and mood of the characters. The windswept moors are violent, vast, and easy to get lost in. Much like the passion between Catherine and Heathcliff, both in their lives and after she dies. The passion doesn't die with her. It extends to the whole family.

JOSEPH: Right! I definitely found myself getting lost in the world of the story.

HENRY: What did you think of Catherine and Heathcliff? I know a lot of people find them unlikable, and I can understand that. But when you realize how betrayed they feel by the other, they become easier to understand.

JOSEPH: They were definitely…melodramatic. Actually, you know what the whole thing kinda reminded me of? A soap opera.

HENRY: *(Wincing ever so slightly)* What?

JOSEPH: Like the scene where Catherine *slaps* Hareton for calling her "wicked aunt Cathy". That's *totally* something that a soap opera diva would do.

HENRY: Soap operas are trashy love stories my mother watches.

JOSEPH: I don't mean it like it's a bad thing. It actually really kept me involved.

HENRY: Have you watched any of the movie versions? Specifically the one from the thirties with Laurence Olivier and Merle Oberon. That version ends when Catherine dies, which some people prefer, but I don't, because Heathcliff's love for Catherine doesn't end at her death.

JOSEPH: I *did* actually watch that version. Honestly, I liked that ending better. Like I still got that Catherine's death didn't stop Heathcliff's love for her, but I didn't need to know about their children or anything. Honestly, the second half of the book felt kinda superfluous to me.

HENRY: It's not superfluous. We need the second half to show how Heathcliff tries to perpetuate his love of Catherine, and his cruelty, through his children and hers. And how the cycle is broken.
It is only when Heathcliff and Catherine and Edgar are all dead, and Hareton and Cathy (the daughter Cathy) get over their differences and marry each other, that there finally peace at Wuthering Heights.

JOSEPH: *("You win...")* Okay.

HENRY: "...and wondered how anyone could ever imagine unquiet slumbers for the sleepers in that quiet earth."
That line still gives me chills.

JOSEPH: That's my boyfriend's favorite final line in any book.

HENRY: Boyfriend?

JOSEPH: Yeah. *Wuthering Heights* is his favorite novel, actually. He's read it six times.

(HENRY snorts.)

HENRY: Only six times? I've read it ninety-five times. Actually ninety-six. I forgot that I read it another time while waiting for you to finish it.

JOSEPH: Six times is still five more times than I've read it.

HENRY: But it's hardly enough to constitute it as your favorite book.

JOSEPH: My favorite book is that *Curious Incident* book. I've only read it once.

HENRY: *The Curious Incident of the Dog in the Night-Time.* You can't even say the *full name*! I haven't even read it and I know the full name.

JOSEPH: So you're saying I don't love something just because I don't feel like saying the *really long* title of a book?

HENRY: You can't love it *that* much.

JOSEPH: Well clearly no one can love *Wuthering Heights* as much as you do.

HENRY: You're right. No one can.

JOSEPH: So why force me to read a book when you're not going to engage in a dialogue about it?

HENRY: I can't engage with ideas that are trivial and imbecilic.

JOSEPH: Well my boyfriend thinks *Wuthering Heights* is like a soap opera, too. And he loves it.

HENRY: Well he's wrong!

(Silence)

JOSEPH: Well.

(JOSEPH pushes the copy of Wuthering Heights *back to* HENRY. HENRY *looks at it.)*

HENRY: You don't want to keep it?

JOSEPH: I'm not gonna read it again. Any time soon, at least.

(A moment. Then HENRY takes the book and puts it in his bag, along with his other copy.)

HENRY: Did you feel a light switch?

JOSEPH: What?

HENRY: When you read *Wuthering Heights.* Did you feel a light switch turn on?

JOSEPH: You mean…did I enjoy it? Yeah. I told you I did.

HENRY: And your boyfriend…I assume he makes you feel a light switch?

(Pause)

JOSEPH: Yeah. He does.

HENRY: Then why did you decide to meet with me? Was it only to tell me you were involved with another?

JOSEPH: *(No point denying it)* Roggie told me to.

HENRY: Roggie?

JOSEPH: Yeah. He came upstate to tell me to read the book. And meet with you. And I don't regret it, Henry. I got to read a really good book out of it.

HENRY: But what do *I* get out of it?

(Pause. JOSEPH sips his coffee. There's no way he can respond.)

HENRY: You told me you only had sex with people you connected with. I thought we did.

JOSEPH: It just happened, Henry. I don't know how else to explain it.

HENRY: I hoped we would be more than one night, Joseph.

Roggie was right about you. You *do* play the field. I should have listened to him.

(*Pause*)

JOSEPH: Look. I'm only telling you this because you said you didn't like false friends or whatever...

HENRY: Or false lovers. Like you.

JOSEPH: Roggie said you were socially retarded.

(*Silence. The words sink in for* HENRY.)

HENRY: What?

JOSEPH: When he came upstate, he said you were "socially retarded".
Which is *really* messed up, considering he was trying to get me to talk to you.

(*Pause*)

HENRY: But. Roggie is my best friend. Best friends don't...
They just don't...

(*A long pause. Perhaps* JOSEPH *regrets telling* HENRY *this.*)

JOSEPH: I'm sorry, Henry. I just thought you should know.

(HENRY *stands up.*)

HENRY: I must take my leave of you.

(*Suddenly, the café and* JOSEPH *disappear, leaving* HENRY *alone in a spotlight.*)

Scene Thirteen

(HENRY, *in the spotlight. We begin hearing voices from the play, one by one, then slowly building on each other, creating a cacophony of sound. He winces as he reacts to each of these.*)

MARIAN: Listen to my tone—

AARON: I *never* wanted to be friends with you!

JOSEPH: So why force me to read a book—

ROGGIE: What you're doing now—

JOSEPH: —when you're not going to engage in a dialogue about it?

ROGGIE: —it's probably making him not want to talk to you.

AARON: I don't want to play with you anymore.
I don't want to play *any game* with you *ever again.*

JOSEPH: I'm not gonna read it again.

MARIAN: You have to talk at other people's levels!

ROGGIE: You know, shoulder to cry on, and all that.

JOSEPH: My boyfriend said—

AARON: Retarded *faggot!*

MARIAN: Do I *sound* like I want to hear you talk!?

KEN: You're impossible. You know that? This whole night, you've just been really…

ROGGIE/JOSEPH: Socially retarded.

AARON: You know the only reason we were friends was because my *mom made me*!?

MARIAN: *Social cues,* Henry!
You should have learned this by now.

MARIAN/JOSEPH: *You should have learned this by now.*

MARIAN/JOSEPH/KEN/AARON: *You should have learned this by now.*

MARIAN/JOSEPH/KEN/AARON/ ROGGIE: *YOU SHOULD HAVE LEARNED THIS BY NOW. YOU SHOULD HAVE LEARNED THIS BY—*

(We hear light switches turning on. HENRY *looks up. The stage lights get brighter and brighter.* ROGGIE's *voice.)*

ROGGIE: I would've *totally* asked you out if you weren't like…

(Then we hear a SWITCH. And the lights shut off, leaving a sliver of light on HENRY.*)*

HENRY: If I wasn't… Just…if I wasn't…

Scene Fourteen

*(*HENRY *is still onstage. He is now in his and* ROGGIE's *apartment.* ROGGIE *look at* HENRY, *who avoids looking at him.)*

ROGGIE: Are you gonna answer me? How'd it go with—

HENRY: You called me socially retarded.
(Pause)
Joseph told me. It was most decent of him to do. Aside from that, our talk went simply horrid. But I don't want to talk about that right now.

ROGGIE: Henry, I—

HENRY: Please shut up and let me talk.
I know that I am not as good with guys as you are, or at people in general. And I know that I'm occasionally awkward, and that I talk weird to some people.
But that does *not* give you the right to tell Joseph, or anyone, that I am socially retarded. And you're not denying it, which sub-textually speaks volumes.

ROGGIE: No, I'm not denying it. I…I wasn't thinking.

I went upstate to ask Joseph to call you back, because I knew that was worrying you. I didn't go there to talk shit about you. Promise.

(HENRY *snorts*.)

HENRY: Thank you for verbally confirming it. This proves you a most false friend indeed.
And a roommate whose cohabitation I'm deeply reconsidering.

ROGGIE: Okay, um…
I understand that you're upset, I said something really stupid, yeah, but we've been roommates for, I don't even *remember* how long.
Can't we talk about this?

(*Long pause.* HENRY *looks at the ground.*)

HENRY: It's not just that you called me socially retarded.

ROGGIE: Okay, then what is it?

HENRY: You said if I wasn't your roommate, you would date me. You said that the night before Valentine's Day, 2011.

ROGGIE: I was wasted that night. I don't remember half the shit I've—

HENRY: (*His eyes don't leave the ground.*) You said you wouldn't date me because I was your roommate.
Which I thought made sense. It was common wisdom not to date our roommates.
You said you would date me if. I'm assuming there is an ellipses at the end of that sentence.
I would have dated you, Roggie.
But you were always off with Jackson, or a multitude of other men, and never once did you ask if I wanted

to be intimate with you. Not only because I was your roommate, but because I was autistic, too.
(He looks up at ROGGIE.*)*
Can you confirm my suspicions?

*(*ROGGIE *takes this in.)*

ROGGIE: We *were* intimate, Henry. All those times you read to me when I was wasted.

HENRY: Did you ever consider that perhaps I wanted another form of intimacy from you?

ROGGIE: I did, but…

HENRY: I was going to bring it up when we were no longer roommates. I thought we would come to some understanding. But then you moved to New York and asked me to be your roommate again. I accepted out of convenience. And we settled nicely together, at least I thought. Even as you slept around and insisted on taking me out to parties where I would fall behind on my reading schedule.

ROGGIE: I just wanted you to have some experience.

HENRY: With *other men*! Not with *you*!

(Silence)

ROGGIE: Is that how you really see me? As just a guy who sleeps around?

HENRY: Yes.

ROGGIE: Maybe…I don't want you to see me that way anymore.

HENRY: What are you proposing I see you as?

ROGGIE: Someone who can make you happy.

HENRY: I don't understand.

ROGGIE: I've…I've just always felt that, if the circumstances were right… If you go, I don't know if…

I...*don't* want you to go.

HENRY: Roggie.

ROGGIE: I'd miss you a lot, Henry. Most ardently.

HENRY: Please, don't. Roggie—

(ROGGIE *goes to* HENRY *and kisses him, square on the mouth. This lasts for a few moments.* HENRY, *to his own surprise, doesn't fight back. They pull away from each other. A moment as they look at each other in the eyes.*)

ROGGIE: I understand you haven't forgiven me for what I said. And I understand that you'll need time. But I'm willing to wait, Henry. However long it takes for you.

HENRY: I...I don't feel the light switch.

(ROGGIE *pulls away, then turns away from* HENRY.)

ROGGIE: Oh... Um...
(*Awkward pause*)
Can you...explain what you mean by...?

HENRY: I was thinking that this would be like Lizzie and Darcy in *Pride and Prejudice,* when she finds out about how he saved her family from ruin and she falls in love with him right there. That perhaps, since you tried to salvage whatever I had with Joseph, I would fall in love with you instead. And perhaps the kiss would confirm our feelings.
But...I don't feel any of that, Roggie. I thought I would. But I don't.
(*Silence*)
I'm going to pack a few of my things. I'll be back for the rest of them tomorrow.
(*He starts to exit.*)

ROGGIE: Henry...

(HENRY *stops.*)

ROGGIE: When you made me read *Wuthering Heights* in college, I enjoyed your explanations more than the book itself.

It... You...flipped on a light switch in me. For...you.

(A moment)

HENRY: I had a light switch for you. But perhaps I spent so long pushing it down that I can never flip it up again.

And from what you're saying, it sounds like I could only flip yours up halfway.

ROGGIE: I just didn't want to...

Do wrong by you. Somehow. Like I didn't want to be like... A Jackson to you.

There was too much I didn't want to mess up. And I messed up anyway...

I'm sorry. For causing you this pain, Henry. It was not intentional.

(...)

Can I at least ask where you're going to stay?

HENRY: I'm going to stay with mama.

ROGGIE: Tell her I say Hi.

HENRY: I won't.

After I tell her what you said about me, she won't give a damn about you. And neither do I.

(He runs offstage.)

ROGGIE: Henry!

(HENRY slams his bedroom door. ROGGIE looks after him. He sits back on the couch and puts his face in his palms.)

Scene Fifteen

(October, 2017. A few hours later. MARIAN's *house in New Jersey.* HENRY *sitting on the couch.* MARIAN *brings out two cups with tea for them.)*

MARIAN: *(Faux-British accent)* Spot of afternoon tea, sir?

HENRY: Thank you.

*(*MARIAN *and* HENRY *sip some tea.)*

MARIAN: How's the semester going?

HENRY: It's good. Busy.

MARIAN: And how's Roggie doing? What's he been up to these days?

HENRY: He's good. He said I was socially retarded.

(He sips his tea.)

MARIAN: What?

HENRY: I heard it from…someone. He said that I was socially retarded.

MARIAN: Are you sure this other person wasn't trying to, I don't know—

HENRY: Perhaps. But I believe him.

MARIAN: Have you talked to Roggie about this, at least?

HENRY: Yes. And he did not deny it.

Other things were said, but I don't want to discuss them. I cannot bear to be in the same space with him anymore. Which brings me to the purpose of my visit: I was wondering if I could perhaps stay with you for a spell.

MARIAN: Of course you can, Henry, but—

HENRY: Thank you.

MARIAN: But you're still gonna be paying rent on—

HENRY: Roggie's going to find a new roommate. I'm sure he's already found a hot young twink on Grindr.

(HENRY's *cell phone rings. It's* ROGGIE. HENRY *shuts it off.*)

HENRY: I do not want to talk to him. He's right, really. As were you.

MARIAN: What?

HENRY: All my life with you it's been, "Social cues", "Social cues", Social cues" because you wanted people to like me.
And I thought it didn't matter, or wouldn't matter, because what care I for social cues? Well guess what. It did matter. And now people think I'm socially retarded.
I cede to you! Congratulations!

MARIAN: I didn't realize we were playing a game, Henry.

(HENRY *stands up.*)

HENRY: Well we were. I apologize for being a profound disappointment of a son—

MARIAN: Sit down.

HENRY: —due to my ignorance of social cues.

MARIAN: Sit down and drink your tea.

HENRY: There's nothing more I can say to you, other than—

MARIAN: *Sit down and drink your fucking tea.*

(*This stops* HENRY. *He sits down and takes a sip of his tea.*)

MARIAN: Now. I'm going to give you ten seconds to breathe and calm down. Then we can talk.

HENRY: That only makes it worse.

MARIAN: Ten seconds.

HENRY: Mama—

MARIAN: I don't hear you breathing.

(Frustrated, HENRY starts breathing. Ten seconds pass. Then he stops.)

MARIAN: Why don't I give you ten more?

(Ten seconds pass. HENRY breathes.)

MARIAN: There. Do you feel better?

HENRY: No.

MARIAN: Drink your tea. Let me know if you want more. Whenever you want to start talking, I'm all ears.

(Moments pass. HENRY and MARIAN drink tea. Whenever HENRY is ready, he starts speaking.)

HENRY: I can't turn on the other light switches.

MARIAN: What other light switches?

HENRY: Other people have many light switches that allow them to talk about many things. I only have the one for 19th Century British Literature. It's the only thing that makes me feel… Incandescent.
But it doesn't make many other people incandescent. Actually, that's not true.
There was this gentleman I was interested in but am not anymore. I loaned him a copy of *Wuthering Heights* to read, and he read it, and I asked if it turned a light switch on in him. I don't think it did. And consequentially, I don't think *I* did. He met another guy who does. He's his boyfriend now.
And I can't help but think it's because of this, this… This *burden* that makes me *socially*…

(HENRY taps his head. He then puts his face in his palms. MARIAN comforts him.)

HENRY: I just want to *understand*.

MARIAN: Shhhh… Shhh…

This guy you mentioned. The one who read *Wuthering Heights*. Can you tell me more about what happened there?

HENRY: Well... We did something that I assume you'd rather not picture me doing.
Then I leant him the book because I wanted him to read it. He took a while to do so, but he did, and we met up at a café to talk about, and it went simply horrid.

MARIAN: What made it horrid?

HENRY: He compared it to a soap opera. Which it's not. It's art. And soap operas aren't. I know you love them, but they're not.

MARIAN: He must have been engaged with the book, if he could make a comparison like that. Right?

HENRY: I suppose...

MARIAN: Sounds like you were able to get someone interested in something you love! That's pretty remarkable, Henry.

HENRY: But we couldn't discuss it. I think it's one way. He thinks it's another.

MARIAN: And you don't think he's allowed to have his own take on it?

HENRY: He is, but does he really love it if he doesn't see it the way that people who love it do?

MARIAN: There's no one way to love something, Henry.

HENRY: But I don't think he *loved* the book. He said he didn't like the second half. Or rather, he said he didn't see the need for it.
How can you love a book if you only love a part of it?

MARIAN: It's like loving a person, I think. I loved your father. There were several parts of him I didn't love. But I still loved the whole person.

HENRY: But he was an impudent bastard and left you.

MARIAN: Yes. But, I forgave him.

HENRY: Because you had to.

MARIAN: No. I forgave him because I had you to raise. And I didn't want you to see me as unforgiving.

HENRY: You said you didn't love parts of my father. Are there parts of me you don't love? It's okay if there are. There are several parts of you I don't love.

MARIAN: Fair enough. Then yes. There are.
But that doesn't mean you're not my son. And that I don't want the best for you. You know, I was telling Sherry— You remember Sherry, right?

HENRY: Shop Rite Sherry?

MARIAN: Yes. She came into the pharmacy to pick up a prescription the other day. And she was telling me about how there are several parents who bring their autistic children shopping with them, and she can tell they're worried. And she tells them about how her friend
Marian has a son who is autistic, and is not only living on his own, but also has his Master's, and is going for his Ph.D at Columbia. And it makes them feel better about their children.

HENRY: But not every autistic child grows up the same, Mama. Perhaps those children will grow up to embody all their parents' fears about them.

MARIAN: Or perhaps they will turn out to be wonderful. Like you, Henry.
When you were diagnosed, the doctors said you wouldn't be able to sustain conversation, or develop

strong relationships. That you would never be able to live on your own. Or drive. Or hold down a job. That you would be very good at math, but not English. I spent nights worrying about how you would turn out. Would you fall in love. Would you have a family. A few years after you were diagnosed—you were six at the time—I took you to the library, because that was the *only* place you wanted to go every Saturday. I signed you up for story time, but you were never interested in that. You would always sneak off to the grown-up books section. I remember, you were reading this *giant* book.

HENRY: *The Woman in White* by Wilkie Collins.

MARIAN: And you were sitting there with it *so intently.* And I thought, "no way he is understanding it." But you asked to check it out, so we did, and you read it that entire week. And every night at dinner, you would quote *direct paragraphs* from the book to me. Do you remember that?

HENRY: Yes.

MARIAN: So when we brought it back to the library, the librarian asked if *I* had enjoyed the book. I told her that *you* had checked it out and read it. And the look on her face, I'll never forget it! You asked her what other books were like it. And she suggested *The Moonstone* to you because it was by the same author as *The Woman in White.* And you read that book in a week, too. And then the librarian suggested to you The Hound of the Baskervilles, and you read that. Then you started finding books on your own, like *Wuthering Heights,* and *Jane Eyre.* And *Pride and Prejudice,* and *Emma*— You had this gift of summarizing these really complicated books that no one your age could read. I may have gotten frustrated when you talked about them so much. But even so, I thought, perhaps my son

could be a book critic. Or an English teacher. Or maybe a writer himself.
And for the first time, I wasn't worried about you.

HENRY: Until I told you I was gay. You worried about me then.

MARIAN: Only for a little while. I knew I had to be supportive, and I think I did a pretty good job in that regard.

HENRY: You did.

(HENRY *puts down his tea and embraces* MARIAN. *A tender moment between them*)

MARIAN: I know you're not feeling good about yourself. But please know that I think you've turned out pretty remarkably.
You are *remarkable*, Henry.

HENRY: Thank you, mommy.

(HENRY *and* MARIAN *separate.* HENRY'*s cell phone rings. He looks at it.*)

HENRY: It's still Roggie.

(*He presses his phone and puts it down.*)

MARIAN: He probably just wants to know where you are.

HENRY: No he doesn't. I told him I was coming here. Oh no. If this means he'll come knocking on the door—

MARIAN: I'll tell him you don't want to see him.

HENRY: Thank you. I don't want to see Roggie ever again.

(MARIAN *sips her tea.*)

HENRY: I sense you have something to say, mama.

MARIAN: I mean, you feel about Roggie however you feel, but...

You said he didn't deny what he said about you. He would be rather duplicitous if he did, right?

HENRY: Excellent use of your vocabulary, mama.

MARIAN: The first time he came over for dinner, he told me you were the most passionate person he knew. And seven years later, he's still your roommate. Henry, so many friendships don't last that long.

HENRY: I suppose...

MARIAN: It sounds like, from what you're saying, he said something he shouldn't have said. But he's not the only one who can say something stupid. Or hurtful. How many people have I heard you describe as imbecilic?

(This gets HENRY. *He can't respond.)*

MARIAN: I just think, if I'm being completely honest, you're being a little unforgiving.

HENRY: I know you want me to forgive him. But please respect that I can't. Not right now. Maybe one day I will. But not now.

MARIAN: Alright. In your own time, then.

(Pause)

HENRY: Do you still have *The Curious Incident of the Dog in the Night-Time*?

MARIAN: You know, as a matter of fact...

*(*MARIAN *goes to a bookshelf and pulls out the book. She gives it to* HENRY.*)*

MARIAN: Does this mean you're finally going to read it?

HENRY: Yes. I believe so.

MARIAN: You'll have to let me know when you finish it.

HENRY: I will.

(MARIAN *picks up the tea mugs and exits with them.*
HENRY *opens* The Curious Incident of the Dog in the
Night-Time *and begins reading.*)

Scene Sixteen

(*The scenery begins to open up. We see a park emerge. It is a
bright, sunny afternoon in April, 2018.*)

(HENRY *finds himself sitting on a bench. He is reading*
Maurice *by E M Forster.*)

(*After a few moments,* ROGGIE *enters dressed in running
clothes. He has earbuds in his ears. He sees* HENRY. ROGGIE
runs past HENRY, *then stops. He then turns around and
looks at* HENRY, *who keeps reading.*)

(ROGGIE *approaches* HENRY.)

ROGGIE: Hey. Henry.

(HENRY *keeps reading. After a few moments, he closes his
book and looks up towards* ROGGIE, *without looking at him
directly in the eye.*)

HENRY: Roggie.

ROGGIE: Finish your chapter?

HENRY: Yes.

ROGGIE: What are you reading?

HENRY: *Maurice* by E M Forster. I've been told I should
read it before.
I thought it was high time I read it to see what all the
fuss was about.

ROGGIE: Cool. Are you going to talk about it on your
channel, or...?

HENRY: No. I only talk about 19th Century British
Literature on my channel.

ROGGIE: Oh…

HENRY: You've watched my channel.

ROGGIE: Yeah. "On the Literary Spectrum."
Your videos are really good, I've watched all of them.

HENRY: Thank you.

ROGGIE: What else have you been reading?

HENRY: Many books written after 1901, if you can
believe it.

ROGGIE: Yeah?

HENRY: I reread *The Great Gatsby*. I read it in high
school, but I was more into reading *North and South*
by Elizabeth Gaskell. So I wanted to know if perhaps I
was missing something.
After I finish *Maurice* I'm going to read *Beloved* by Toni
Morrison.

ROGGIE: I've heard good things about that one.

HENRY: As have I.

ROGGIE: Are you still at your mom's house, or…?

HENRY: Yes. I still reside there.

ROGGIE: I thought about going out there to check in on
you, but I figured you needed space.

HENRY: Much appreciated.
And how's the apartment?
Did Grindr provide you a satisfactory roommate?

ROGGIE: Actually, my roommate is a girl.
She's a friend of my sister's. She's doing an internship
and needed somewhere to stay.
It was funny, I saw her reading *Wuthering Heights*
and she called it sexist trash. We had a *looooong*
conversation about it.

HENRY: The female characters in that book are rather horrible...

ROGGIE: You know, since you moved out six months ago, I've been doing some reading myself.

HENRY: Yes, Roggie. Masturbating to gay erotica counts as reading.

(ROGGIE *laughs.*)

ROGGIE: No, actually.

(ROGGIE *shows* HENRY *his iPhone.*)

HENRY: *Jane Eyre.*

ROGGIE: I've been making my way through the audiobook of it. I'm on the last chapter. It makes me think of you.
Like, even though it's a woman narrating, I hear you saying everything in here.

HENRY: I confess, Roggie, you've been occupying my thoughts as well.

ROGGIE: Really?

HENRY: Yes.
I re-watched your videos on your channel. Voluntarily.

ROGGIE: *All* of them?

HENRY: Yes. I was most struck by the one about giving people chances.
Because you never know if you'll be able to have the same experience with them ever again.

ROGGIE: Yeah, that's probably the video I'm the proudest of.
I'm glad you're re-watching them, Henry. That makes me...happy.
(Pause)
You know, uh...
Listening to *Jane Eyre,* it's kinda messed up.

Jane finds out Rochester has hidden his wife in an attic, and she says she forgives him on the spot. Just like that.

HENRY: "Reader, I forgave him at the moment and on the spot. There was such deep remorse in his eye, such true pity in his tone, such manly energy in his manner; and besides, there was such unchanged love in his whole look and mien—I forgave him all: yet not in words, not outwardly; only at my heart's core."

ROGGIE: Yeah. I would be like, Nope! You know? But Jane goes back to him.

HENRY: It's an example of Passion versus Reason. Jane loves Rochester, but she knows she can't allow herself to be attached to a man who couldn't detach himself from another woman and furthermore would not convey this part of his life to her. She forgives him but she doesn't trust him.

ROGGIE: Right. And there was another quote, when she's with that Rivers guy...

HENRY: "Both by nature and principle, he was superior to the mean gratification of vengeance: he had forgiven me for saying I scorned him and his love, but he had not forgotten the words; and as long as he and I lived he never would forget them."

ROGGIE: How do you do that?

HENRY: I've read the book fifty-seven times.

ROGGIE: But like, you knew *exactly* which quotes I was going to use. That's...eerie.

HENRY: No it's not. I'm just able to remember them at this particular moment.

ROGGIE: But if Jane can forgive Rochester. I mean, I guess I just wondered if maybe you'd thought about...

(Silence)

HENRY: Why did you kiss me?

(ROGGIE *thinks of what he should say.*)

ROGGIE: Because...
It felt right. In the moment. Because I wanted to.
And I thought you'd maybe wanted it, too.

HENRY: I don't want you to kiss me now.

ROGGIE: I wasn't going to.

(Pause)

HENRY: Passion vs. Reason. I feel a lot of passion over
how you should not have called me socially retarded
behind my back.

ROGGIE: I understand.

HENRY: However. Reason. We *have* been roommates for
seven years.
And you've already kissed me, and I felt nothing,
which signifies that I don't pine after you anymore.

ROGGIE: So...?

(Long pause)

HENRY: I could offer words of forgiveness. But I fear
they should ring hollow. I want to mean them.

ROGGIE: Well. I forgive you, Henry.

HENRY: What for?

ROGGIE: Abruptly moving out and making me have to
find another roommate, for one thing.

HENRY: You found another one quick enough.

ROGGIE: But mostly for calling me a false friend.
I said something stupid. I shouldn't have said it. I own
up to that. But that one stupid thing can't ruin *seven
years* of friendship.
Hell, I wouldn't spend seven years as your roommate
if I didn't feel like we...fit in some way.

HENRY: I felt we fit too.

ROGGIE: I just want us to be okay again. I don't care if we're roommates, or boyfriends, or lovers, I just want us to be okay.

HENRY: I suppose the only way we'll ever be okay is if I forgive you.

ROGGIE: It would be a start.
You know I made a video about this too, right? Knowing when to forgive someone? I know you watched it.

HENRY: "You aren't obligated to forgive someone. But if they add value to your life, and the good outweighs the bad, and your life would be worse without them, then you should consider it."

ROGGIE: Exactly. You add value to my life, Henry. I like to think I add value to yours.

HENRY: I rather enjoyed the private underwear modeling you'd do for me.

(ROGGIE *laughs*.)

ROGGIE: I hope I add more value than that.

HENRY: I must admit, I have been thinking that I will miss our weekends upstate. I did enjoy reading by the lake.
And you badgering me to go to sex parties where I would meet people who would end up disappointing me.

ROGGIE: I know Joseph didn't work out.
But you might meet someone else who will. You never know.

(HENRY *thinks. Then:*)

HENRY: Look at me.

ROGGIE: Okay.

(HENRY *and* ROGGIE *look at each other for a long, long
moment. This is the first time* HENRY *has looked directly
at* ROGGIE *throughout the whole scene.* HENRY *sees the
remorse in* ROGGIE'*s eyes.)*

HENRY: I forgive you, Roggie.
I forgive you for calling me socially retarded behind
my back while you were trying to get Joseph to talk to
me.

ROGGIE: Thank you, Henry.

HENRY: But I won't forget.

ROGGIE: Neither will I.
I will do better, though. I promise.

HENRY: As will I.

(*Pause.* HENRY *and* ROGGIE *take in the scene around them.)*

ROGGIE: "It will atone… It will atone."

HENRY: "It will atone."

(*A new light switch flips on in both* HENRY *and* ROGGIE.
Blackout)

END OF PLAY